To Roberta)

All good wishes!

Bruce Tannabrandt

My Name Is On The Deed…

But The Cats Own The House

Bruce S. Garrabrandt

Other books by Bruce Garrabrandt

The Power of Having Desire

Cattle Drive

(And 153 Other Random Acts of Artistic Nonsense)

For Ruth Soulier — a woman with nine lives.

Acknowledgements

Special thanks to Jeffrey White, of White Custom Media, for transforming my words and art into this playful gift book. His creative artistry touches every page.

Kudos also go to the following people, whose cat photos and/or title suggestions provided models and inspiration for me at the easel: Richard Ball, Betsy and Scott Brown, Jan Garrabrandt (who urged me to create this book), Lynne Griffin, John and Carol Hoff, Bob Iwig, Janet Johnson, Paul McCullough, Jessica Sarlin, Laura Siess, Paula Tilisky, Amber and Bryan Wise, and Jean Woolley.

Introduction

People who don't like cats haven't met the right cat. Once that connection is made, non-cat people are charmed by feline affection and become putty in their paws.

"Cats are unfriendly" is a common misconception held by unbelievers. That's understandable. Usually, their only exposure to cats comes while visiting a cat owner's home, where the animal takes one look at them—this stranger invading its territory—and immediately darts under the couch.

With their owners, cats exhibit a warmth and dependence that outsiders cannot possibly know. It is a special bond—well worth cultivating. Cats also provide ongoing entertainment for their human companions. Their quirky behaviors bring us lots of smiles. I hope to have captured some of these moments for you in the following pages.

Sleeper Sofa

Cats keep our egos in check. When you ask a dog to do something, it responds to your demands instantly. Cats generally stare at you with a look that says, "Why? I'm comfortable where I am."

There are exceptions, of course. Callie, pictured on the opposite page, is best described as "a head in search of a hand." She lives to have her ears and chin scratched. Lower your hand to the floor and motion for her to come to you and—regardless how deeply she's embedded among the pillows—Callie will saché over to you for petting purposes.

But here's the deal: She expects you to keep petting her. Take your hand away from her head and Callie looks up at you—as if to ask, "That's it? You mean I hauled myself off the sofa for a tease?" Guiltily you resume the petting, eliciting a satisfied purr of thanks from Callie.

TEN COMMON FACTS EVERY CAT KNOWS

1. No matter how many water bowls you place around the house, I'll still drink from your Christmas tree stand.

2. I will usually sleep when you want me to play, and play when you prefer that I sleep.

3. You, on the other hand, will sleep only when I want you to sleep and play when I want you to play.

4. Endearing tricks performed by me—such as fetching a catnip mouse—will never be demonstrated in front of your friends. Repeated pleadings by you will be met by blank stares from me—and probably from your friends.

5. Anything in your home moveable by my paw will eventually be a cat toy.

6. All pens belong on the floor—preferably under the sofa or in other places hard to reach by you.

7. The best time to pet me each day is now.

8. Any friend of yours is not necessarily a friend of mine, unless that person brings me treats.

9. Your house has as many beds in it as it does open drawers, empty boxes and, of course, beds.

10. God's primary purpose in giving you the ability to sit down was to create a lap.

Bathroom Attendant

My original title for this drawing was *Be Discreet—You Never Know Who's Watching.* The image features the rear portion of Jack, a recent feline addition to The Artist's Inn.

Because many people are allergic to pet dander, our cats are not allowed into the guest rooms at the bed-and-breakfast; however, this house rule is repeatedly broken as guests secretly invite the cats in—as temporary roommates—when we're not looking.

The idea for *Bathroom Attendant* came from a photograph taken by a couple who stayed with us in 2008. (The photo was tucked inside their Christmas card to us.) Here was clear evidence that, not only did Jack gain access to the guests' room, but also made his way into their bath. My initial reaction to the photo was one of embarrassment, but this quickly gave way to inspiration and, ultimately, to the drawing you see here.

Jack is, by far, the most outgoing of our four cats. He can make his presence known from anywhere in the house with his loud, peculiar purr. The sound is a cross between that of a frog and a pigeon. I guess Jack is our resident "Frigeon." His cartoon purr, happy disposition, and affectionate greeting to everyone he sees are traits that endear him as a delightful new member of our family.

21 Paths to

The Purrfect Life…

Door Jam

1. Attempt the impossible.

Copy Cat

2. Cultivate your curiosity.

Parenthesis

3. Get plenty of sleep.

4. Accept challenges with determination.

What's the Scoop?

5. Find a creative use for everything.

Catsup in the Fridge

6. Get out of your comfort zone.

Curtain Call

7. Be courageous and take a leap.

Gluttony—a Cardinal Sin

8. Dream.

Cattitude

9. Express yourself honestly.

Under The Weather

10. Get plenty of sleep.

No Depawsit/No Return

11. Make the time and place each day for quiet solitude. Embrace contemplation.

Go Green - Eat Catnip

12. Savor life's simple pleasures.

One Topping Too Many

13. Practice moderation in all things…including moderation.

Shelf Life

14. Occasionally take a detached view. Find a perch from which you can calmly observe your surroundings.

Up to No Good

15. Keep a playful attitude.

Windowbox and Whiskers

16. Be patient and pay attention. Something worthwhile will come into view.

Water Bed

17. Learn to be comfortable anywhere.

Catastrophies

18. Get plenty of sleep.

©2009 B. GARRABRANDT

46

19. Don't be afraid to look silly.

Business Partner

20. Put yourself into your work–or, at least rest and think about it.

Cat Yoga Positions

21. Get plenty of sleep.

A Tribute To Pongo

For ten years, Pongo belonged to our next-door neighbors, initially a birthday present to their six-year-old daughter. A decade later, the now 16-year-old teenager had other interests. Pongo spent most of his time alone outside. He tried to make friends with the local cats, but these were feral, farm animals who only hissed and threatened when he made friendly overtures.

Pongo passed his days snoozing in my wife Jan's flowerbeds, and keeping her company while she weeded the garden. He'd roll over onto his back to watch her, upside down, as she worked in the soil. (Jan only tolerates me—but she loved Pongo. He captivated her with his dreamy eyes and sweet disposition.)

One morning while preparing breakfast, Jan glanced out the kitchen window to see a dead cat in the middle of Main Street. Her eyes filled with tears. She called me into the kitchen with the words, "I think Pongo's been killed by a car." I walked outside for a closer look. It wasn't Pongo.

Later we found him sunbathing in our side yard. That was the day Pongo became an indoor cat—and our official greeter at The Artist's Inn.

He took to his new home immediately. He loved welcoming guests, winning them over instantly with his warm purr, earnestly coaxing them to disregard our "no cats allowed in the guest rooms" policy.

On nights when Pongo couldn't be found, we assumed he was upstairs with guests, curled at the foot of their bed. Suspicions were always confirmed in the pre-dawn hours of the following morning, when the patter of Pongo's feet were heard on the stairs as he trotted down to meet the new day on our dining room windowsill.

Closed guest room doors were never a challenge for him. Standing on his hind legs, he'd place a paw on either side of the door knob and jiggle it until the latch released from the jamb. Then he'd lean his weight against the door and open it. "We thought you had ghosts," guests would tell us at breakfast the next morning, "—but it was just Pongo, strolling in to visit."

He remained a happy, loving fixture at the inn for five years. In August, 2008, an allergic reaction to an anesthetic, administered for a routine test, took Pongo from us. He was fifteen.

In September, a buff-colored kitten appeared in our neighborhood, looking for a home. We dubbed her "Chardonnay" and adopted her. A week later, her brother arrived on our side porch and peered in the window at guests during breakfast. He joined our feline family that morning. His name is Jack.

Perhaps these kittens were sent to us by the spirit of Pongo, who concluded that it would take two cats to replace him. If so, then our departed friend was wrong—he is irreplaceable.

FIVE REQUESTS FROM YOUR CAT

1. Please understand that I always prefer to be on the other side of any closed door in the house.

2. Opened newspapers and magazines are not designed for reading. These are primarily invitations for me to stop and rest awhile.

3. You may identify yourself with a particular career, but realize that I see your official title as Litter Control Engineer.

4. If the cans you open in the kitchen don't contain food for me, please be courteous and use a manual can opener so that I can't hear you. Otherwise, I'll come running—only to be disappointed.

5. I agree not to hold a grudge against you for having neutered me, so long as you pledge to pamper me properly.

Played Out

Postscript from the Inn Cats

Should your future travel plans include a trip to Lancaster County, PA, we invite you to stay at The Artist's Inn. During your visit, be sure to request an audience with us. We spend most of every day power napping in our private quarters, but would welcome the opportunity to be fussed over by you in the sitting room.

Feel free to bring us cat toys. (Don't tell the innkeepers, though—they'd be livid.) One of our repeat guests, originally from Jamaica, says there's an expression down there to describe proper etiquette when visiting another's home: "Don't go there with your arms swinging." We suggest that you fill your arms with toy mice. They're a big hit with us. Sure, we already have lots of them here, but their tails have been bitten off and we can't remember where we've hidden most of them.

Don't bother to bring us catnip, because the innkeepers grow it for us in their herb garden. Actually, catnip has pretty much taken over the herb garden, so you're welcome to take some home for your feline family members. Believe us—it's potent stuff! They'll love you for it.

Oh—one final thought…about the innkeepers' rule that no cats be allowed in the guest rooms: Should you choose to violate this inn policy, your secret is safe with us.

Some of the drawings featured in this book are available as limited edition, signed/numbered lithographs. To view these colored pencil images and many others (both whimsical and traditional), visit Bruce Garrabrandt's website:

http://www.artbybruce.com